RACIAL LITERACY

Examining Assimilation

Emilly Prado

Enslow Publishing
101 W. 23rd Street
Suite 240
New York, NY 10011
USA
enslow.com

LONGWOOD PUBLIC LIBRARY

Published in 2019 by Enslow Publishing, LLC.
101 W. 23rd Street, Suite 240, New York, NY 10011

Copyright © 2019 by Enslow Publishing, LLC.

All rights reserved.

No part of this book may be reproduced by any means without the written permission of the publisher.

Library of Congress Cataloging-in-Publication Data

Names: Prado, Emilly, author.
Title: Examining assimilation / Emilly Prado.
Description: New York : Enslow Publishing, 2019. | Series: Racial literacy | Includes bibliographical references and index. | Audience: Grades 7–12. | Identifiers: LCCN 2018015221| ISBN 9781978504691 (library bound) | ISBN 9781978505643 (pbk.)
Subjects: LCSH: Immigrants—United States—Juvenile literature. | Immigrants—Cultural assimilation—Juvenile literature. | Americanization—Juvenile literature. | United States—Emigration and immigration—Juvenile literature. | United States—Race relations—Juvenile literature.
Classification: LCC E184.A1 P668 2019 | DDC 305.800973—dc23
LC record available at https://lccn.loc.gov/2018015221

Printed in the United States of America

To Our Readers: We have done our best to make sure all website addresses in this book were active and appropriate when we went to press. However, the author and the publisher have no control over and assume no liability for the material available on those websites or on any websites they may link to. Any comments or suggestions can be sent by email to customerservice@enslow.com.

Photo Credits: Cover, p. 1 Golden Pixels LLC/Alamy Stock Photo; p. 6 Rawpixel.com/Shutterstock.com; p. 7 Interim Archives/Archive Photos/Getty Images; p. 11 GL Archive/Alamy Stock Photo; p. 13 PHAS/Universal Images Group/Getty Images; p. 14 Alex Peña/LatinContent Editorial/Getty Images; p. 17 spatuletail/Shutterstock.com; pp. 20, 39 Bettmann/Getty Images; p. 22 National Geographic Creative/Bridgeman Images; p. 25 Ed Vebell/Archive Photos/Getty Images; p. 27 Hulton Archive/Archive Photos/Getty Images; p. 29 Fotosearch/Archive Photos/Getty Images; p. 32 Prakash Mathema/AFP/Getty Images; p. 34 Dickinson College Archives & Special Collections; p. 36 William Thomas Cain/Getty Images; p. 38 Eliot Elisofon/The LIFE Picture Collection/Getty Images; p. 43 PR Image Factory/Shutterstock.com; p. 46 Richard Levine/Alamy Stock Photo; p. 47 Noam Galai/WireImage/Getty Images; p. 49 Alex Halada/AFP/Getty Images; p. 51 Blend Images/Alamy Stock Photo; p. 52 © AP Images; p. 55 © iStockphoto.com/SolStock; p. 57 Salim October/Shutterstock.com; p. 59 India Picture/Shutterstock.com; p. 60 Tassii/E+/Getty Images; p. 63 Zurijeta/Shutterstock.com; p. 65 Ken Huang/Stone/Getty Images; p. 66 Danny Feld/©The CW Network/courtesy Everett Collection; p. 68 Monkey Business Images/Shutterstock.com; cover and interior pages background design Ensuper/Shutterstock.com (colors), Miloje/Shutterstock.com (texture).

CONTENTS

Introduction 5

1 What Is Assimilation? 9

2 Changing American Borders and Identities 19

3 Outlawing the Other 30

4 Why We Assimilate 41

5 A Culture of Assimilation 50

6 How to Combat Assimilation 62

Chapter Notes 70

Glossary 77

Further Reading 78

Index 79

Introduction

If you're a student in the United States, chances are you've felt the need to fit in at some point in your life. But have you ever thought about what it means to fit in and where the idea comes from? Although there are many different ways people in society try to fit in, a common way people discuss fitting in is by using the idea of assimilation as it relates to culture, immigration, and the American identity. Assimilation is the process of adapting or becoming similar to something.

As the United States has changed and grown older, ideas of assimilation have shifted. Earlier models of assimilation ideas, or theories, such as classic/new assimilation models, date back to the early 1900s. These models focus on the idea that immigrants will become more similar to the dominant culture as time goes on. The 1908 play *The Melting Pot* by Israel Zangwill popularized the phrase "melting pot" as it relates to cultural assimilation and was used widely by politicians and citizens alike.

Examining Assimilation

More than 43.7 million immigrants live in the United States today, making up 13.5 percent of the population.

Like soup or fondue, the "melting pot" became a metaphor used to describe the United States as a fused blend of people. Those who believe in the idea of classic assimilation think there's a point when all immigrants can become "fully" assimilated and accepted, and they consider complete assimilation a good thing. With the rise of the civil rights movement, however, a new theory of assimilation formed. The racial/ethnic disadvantage model argues that discrimination against people of color prevents "full assimilation." This model takes into consideration examples of people who adopt the language of their new country and behave in ways that are in line with "American values," but are still treated as less than equal. Segmented assimilation was another popular model in the 1990s that saw assimilation as a process with

Introduction

many factors and a more complicated path than simply "fully assimilated" or not.

To completely understand assimilation today, we must consider what the end point of assimilation might be and at what cost. By looking at the history of immigrants, refugees, and people of color in US history as well as the country's shifting borders, we can trace how the ideas that affect identity today have changed over time. Similarly, we can better understand how our own parents, grandparents, and great-grandparents may have been affected by assimilation in the past.

Immigrants arrive at Ellis Island in New York by sea in the early twentieth century.

Examining Assimilation

Even today, cultural assimilation affects our everyday lives. Although the influences of cultural assimilation may not always be obvious, the United States continues to push for one ideal "American identity." By better understanding racist laws that have targeted ethnic, religious, racial, and sexual minorities and the stigma marginalized communities face today, we can examine the relationship people have with themselves, their families, and outside of their homes and consider the influences of a centuries-long belief of cultural assimilation.

CHAPTER 1

What Is Assimilation?

In the United States and beyond, cultural assimilation is often used as a way to talk about how immigrants and refugees adjust to the culture of their new country. Another way to think about cultural assimilation is that it's a way that some people judge how well immigrants fit in with the majority of the population and culture.

While the United States is a diverse country made up of people from many different races and ethnicities, the US Census (a government organization and survey that counts every resident in the country) estimates that, as of 2016, about 61.3 percent of the United States' population identifies as white.[1] As whites are the largest racial group in the United States at two-thirds, they are often referred to as the "dominant" or "majority" population. People who identify as Asian, Black or African American, Native American or Alaska Native, Latinx or Hispanic, or multiracial, are considered "non-dominant" or "minority" populations. Even though the US Census

Examining Assimilation

estimates that by 2044, "more than half of all Americans are projected to belong to a minority group," when looking at cultural assimilation, immigrants in the US are expected to assimilate, or fit in, with the dominant culture which is that of whites.[2]

One phrase that some people in the United States may have heard from media outlets like television and newspapers, or in classrooms is, "The United States is a nation of immigrants." The phrase was made famous by President John F. Kennedy in his 1963 book, *A Nation of Immigrants*, and celebrates multiculturalism and immigrants.[3] While people use this as a reminder of the United States' history and of the Europeans who arrived centuries before, that phrase doesn't tell the full story of the United States or how the country became the diverse nation that it is today. It's important to look at the history of the United States and how it was formed to understand where the idea of assimilation came from, what it means to be an American, and what both ideas mean for people living in the country today.

Mapping the Americas

Before Christopher Columbus reached North America in 1492, indigenous people (later called Native Americans) had already lived on the land for tens of thousands of years. Christopher Columbus traveled around the world on behalf of the Spanish kingdom in search of spices, gold, and other goods that were brought back to Europe to sell. Although the Norse Viking, Leif Erikson, had landed on North America in the 11th century, he gave up trying to colonize the land.[4]

What Is Assimilation?

A painting of Norse explorer Leif Erikson

Examining Assimilation

However, after Columbus made four voyages between the years of 1492 and 1502, the journeys ultimately made the North American continent well known in Europe and sparked an era of even more expeditions.

Following Columbus' voyages, additional wealthy European kingdoms from countries such as England, Portugal, and France ordered their own expeditions to the Americas so they could conquer and establish new colonies. Conquests, which rely on military force and power to take control of a place or group of people against their will, made it possible for Europeans to settle in the Americas because they could use their power to fight the native peoples who were already living there and take over their land.

The Americas span what is known today as the continents of North America and South America. Although, before they were conquered, they were called other names by the people who lived there. By the mid-sixteenth century, Spain had forcibly taken control of large areas within the Americas that had once belonged to the Aztec Kingdom, Inca Empire, and other smaller tribes along southern North America, Central America, western South America, and areas of the Caribbean. Meanwhile, Portugal conquered regions in North America and eastern South America.[5]

This period of conquering and colonizing in history is often referred to in textbooks as the "Age of Discovery" by European historians, but this point of view doesn't consider the pain and destruction experienced by indigenous peoples and their descendants. Even though the "Age of Discovery" began with Columbus' voyages in the fifteenth century,

What Is Assimilation?

A painting of Spanish conquistadors invading indigenous lands during the Battle of Otumba in 1520

the process continued through the end of the eighteenth century, which means over three hundred years of these battles for land and control. Beyond the Americas, Europeans continued to sail to other continents of the world including Africa, Asia, and Australia to repeat the same practices. One of the main goals of this period for European colonizers was to create a worldwide network of trade (buying and selling goods) and a global map to ultimately increase the wealth and power of the European kingdoms. However, as the European kingdoms grew richer as they discovered new places to live and new things to sell, they were able to do so by stealing the land and resources of indigenous people

Examining Assimilation

Indigenous Peoples' Day

Christopher Columbus Day became a national holiday in 1937. Although Columbus is credited with "discovering" the Americas, indigenous people lived on the land for thousands of years prior. The holiday was promoted as a way to reduce ethnic and religious stigma against Italians and Catholics, but for indigenous and Native Americans, it gravely overlooks the painful, traumatic, and violent realities of the history.

Indigenous Peoples' Day was first proposed as an alternative to Columbus Day in 1977. In 1990, South Dakota became the first state in the United States to officially replace it with Native American Day. By 1992, Berkeley, California, was the first city to adopt Indigenous Peoples' Day. As of 2017, over 50 cities and four states have joined in the alternative celebration.

Indigenous Peoples' Day celebrations, like this one in El Salvador in 2016, honor tribes from all nations.

What Is Assimilation?

who didn't have the weapons to protect themselves against the guns of the Europeans.

Atlantic Slave Trade

As the European empires continued to colonize lands around the world, the wealthy people of these nations were able to buy and sell things that they had never seen before. Europeans had always been able to grow plants and crops native to Europe like onions, apples, and wheat, but they were now able to grow and purchase plants that had only grown within the Americas at the time. Plants native to the Americas include corn, vanilla, cacao (what chocolate is made from), and much more. Animals such as horses and cows were also traded to and from the new and old colonies.[6]

With the growing demand for crops and other goods like clothing, the European colonies were struggling to keep up with the work of growing and making all of these items. They wanted to earn as much money as they could to pay for their expeditions and expansion so they would become more powerful. Beginning with the Portuguese in 1526, European nations started to capture and enslave people from the continent of Africa.[7] Europeans destroyed the homes and villages of families and communities in Africa, and chained the people they captured with heavy, painful shackles so they couldn't run away. After that, they would force the people onto ships, so they could be bought and sold.

The European colonizers thought of the African people they kidnapped as property rather than as human beings. European rulers used African people to perform labor, or

Examining Assimilation

work, without any pay. African slaves were treated cruelly and violently by slave-owners. This period of mass African enslavement is called the Atlantic Slave Trade and it happened from the 1500s through the late 1800s. It is estimated that of the 12.5 million African people who were forcibly enslaved during this time, at least 1.5 million died while aboard the ships and many more died shortly after due to harsh conditions, illness, and severe violence.[8] To give a better idea of how many African people were enslaved, New York City (the biggest city in the United States) had a population of just over 8 million people in 2010 while Los Angeles was just under 4 million.

The United States of America Is Born

European nations had been taking over different areas of land across the world for hundreds of years after Christopher Columbus' expeditions. In North America, thirteen settlements controlled by the British occupied the eastern coast of what is now known as the United States. The people living in the colonies had accepted the rules made by the British and even fought wars on their behalf, but the citizens became increasingly unhappy with the lack of control they had in their lives. When the British tried to raise taxes (money paid by the citizens to the government for their services), the thirteen colonies announced their decision to be independent from the British and make the rules of their own country together. With help from the French army, these colonies defeated the British. The Continental Congress

What Is Assimilation?

declared independence from Britain and became the United States of America in 1776.[9]

When the United States became its own country, the main leaders of the independence movement—known as the Founding Fathers—created a constitution. The Constitution is a document that identified the new nation's beliefs and values, and it continues to influence the way the United States is run today. The main beliefs from the Constitution are loyalty, democracy, and faith.

Loyalty within the Constitution is the idea that countrymen must be willing to fight to protect the United States and stand up for their beliefs. They should be patriotic, or proud

Did you know the US Constitution is the oldest national constitution in the world?

Examining Assimilation

of their country, and agree to teach their children the same values. Democracy, on the other hand, focused on supporting the people. Where the British made the rules and enjoyed the luxuries of their riches, people in the colonies were poor and struggling. As a result, the United States decided to have laws chosen for and by the people. It is very important to note, however, that only white people were considered citizens and Black Americans would still be considered property until 100 years later. Faith and a belief in God through Protestant Christianity were also important to the United States.

It's important to read and understand the Constitution because it defines what the United States' first citizens cared about and wanted for their country. Many Americans today still strongly believe in the values of the Constitution as it was written then and use it to evaluate how American someone is now. Since cultural assimilation encourages immigrants to fit in with the dominant group, the values in the Constitution can be considered the jumping off point for understanding the American identity and what it means to be American.

CHAPTER 2

Changing American Borders and Identities

The United States has continued to change rapidly as a country since it was created. From the very beginning, large numbers of European immigrants migrated to the United States and wanted to make the new country their home. To keep up with the growing population, the government decided to take control of more land and expand its borders. While there were various wars and treaties (also known as contracts) that contributed to the United States' growth, the two largest incidents are the Louisiana Purchase and Treaty of Hidalgo. Later, even after slavery was made illegal and the fifty states were formed, the government continued to push the ideals of the original Constitution onto its citizens.

Western Expansion and Shifting Borders

In 1803, nearly half of what is now the United States was controlled by France and inhabited by many Native

Examining Assimilation

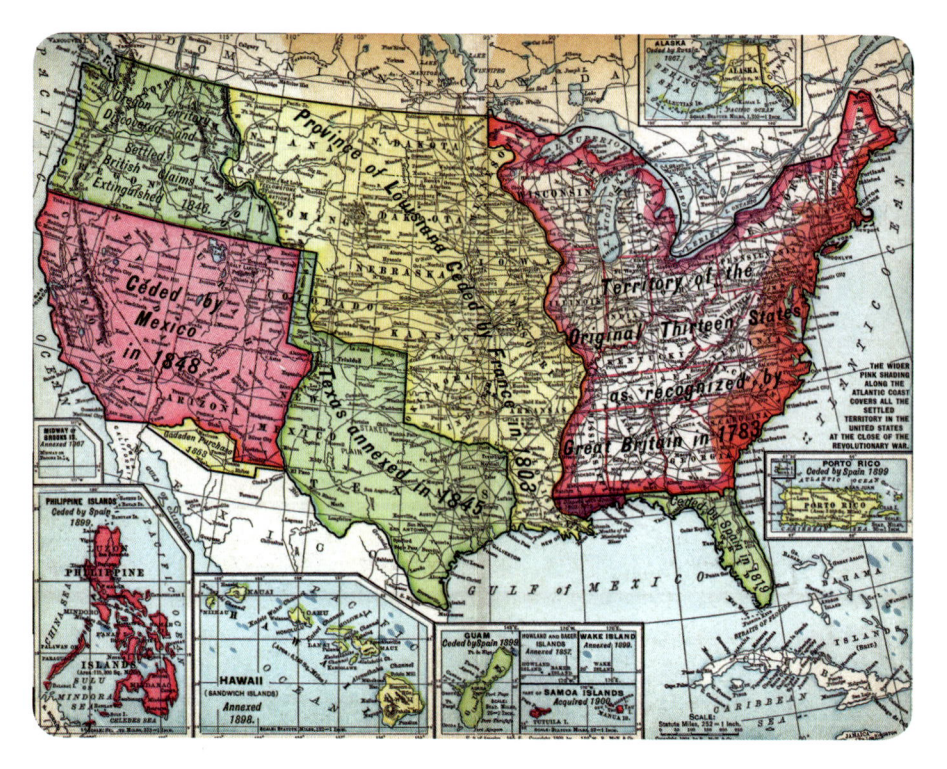

United States' territorial expansion throughout history.

American tribes. In a hasty deal with France, the US government bought the land and doubled its size overnight.[1] Known as the Louisiana Purchase, the contract made it so the United States' population of European descendants could live freely, while pushing out the existing Native American tribes to the territory west of the Mississippi River. Nearly 125,000 Native Americans lived in the area at the time of the Louisiana Purchase. White Americans were fearful of Native Americans simply because their customs, traditions, and people looked different from their own. President George Washington and other leaders in power during the early years of the United States led social campaigns to "civilize" the Native Americans by making them adopt the English language, Christianity, and the capitalistic model of economics.

President Andrew Jackson formalized the plan to create the United States as a country for only White Americans in 1830 by signing the Indian Removal Act into law.[2] At this time in history, Native Americans were still widely referred to as Indians because Christopher Columbus thought he had landed in India. The Indian Removal Act allowed the president to forcibly trade lands in the West in exchange for the existing land of the Native Americans east of the Mississippi. In other words, Native American tribes had to sell the land their homes and communities were on, in "exchange" for a distant, unknown land. The Choctaw, Chickasaw, Seminole, Creek, and Cherokee tribes were primarily affected by this decision. Although some tribes agreed to leave, many didn't and resisted.[3]

Instead of starting a war with weapons, the Cherokee undertook a legal battle by filing a case against the state of Georgia where their lands were. They assimilated to the United States' system for law to try and find a solution that would be honored. When the case reached the US Supreme Court, the judges ruled in favor of the Cherokee and in support of their protected lands. Native Americans' lands were determined sovereign and independent, meaning they were supposed to have the power and control of their own government apart from the United States.[4] But even after losing the case in court, President Jackson and the US army

Examining Assimilation

continued to ignore the law and embarked on a mass eviction of Indian tribes.

By 1839, the United States government had forced the remaining Cherokees and other Native American tribes to move west by making them march some 1,200 miles on foot. This series of forced relocations included the Cherokee removal—known as the Trail of Tears—which resulted in the deaths of thousands of Native Americans, with an estimated 4,000 of 16,000 Cherokee dying. These cruel decisions, however, were justified from the perspective of Andrew

Over one hundred thousand Native Americans were forced by the US government to leave their homes.

Jackson and other white colonizers who believed that the United States' expansion was in line with manifest destiny— the idea rooted in the Constitution that the process was inevitable and encouraged by God.[5]

The 1848 Treaty of Guadalupe Hidalgo is another example of shifting borders. Before the Mexican-American War began in 1846, Mexico had allowed US citizens into their northernmost territories where California and Texas are today to encourage development and economic growth, or wealth. Similarly, to the US Constitution, Mexico required its citizens to be loyal to their country and adopt a religion. Instead of Protestant Christianity, Mexico practiced Roman Catholicism.

By 1830, Texas had a population of 4,000 Mexican Tejanos and 10,000 white Americans.[6] When Texas decided to revolt and seek independence, they became the Republic of Texas in 1836. As the United States continued to seek expansion, tensions rose along the border between Mexico and the Republic of Texas. When a group of US soldiers were attacked by Mexican troops after an alleged robbery, US President James K. Polk declared war. The Mexican-American War lasted for two years until it ended in 1848 with the signing of the Treaty of Guadalupe Hidalgo. The US Army had reached the capitol of Mexico City ready to take over, but the soldiers used this opportunity instead to force Mexico into selling their land. After the treaty was signed, between 75,000 to 100,000 Spanish-speaking Mexicans and 150,000 Native Americans were suddenly living within US borders.[7] Although the treaty promised its new residents citizenship, it would take nearly

Examining Assimilation

100 more years, until the 1930s, for former Mexican citizens to gain full US citizenship.[8]

The End of Slavery

After the Mexican-American War, the US government grew more concerned with slavery and the division it was creating in the country. The majority of white Americans in the southern states relied on slave labor and were pro-slavery, while a small group called abolitionists in the North saw slavery as immoral and sinful. Ultimately, a civil war within the United States broke out in 1861 that lasted four years after Abraham Lincoln was elected president in 1860. In a public letter written in 1862 by President Abraham Lincoln, he explained his views on the war:

> My paramount object in this struggle is to save the Union, and is not either to save or destroy Slavery. If I could save the Union without freeing any slave, I would do it, and if I could save it by freeing all the slaves, I would do it, and if I could save it by freeing some and leaving others alone, I would also do that. What I do about Slavery and the colored race, I do because I believe it helps to save this Union, and what I forbear, I forbear because I do not believe it would help to save the Union.[9]

Still, President Lincoln announced the Emancipation Proclamation, an executive order that freed over 3 million enslaved Black Americans of all ages from control, in 1863. It would take until June 19, 1865 for Texas to learn of the news—a date that is celebrated today as the end of slavery called Juneteenth. Since the proclamation didn't apply to all

Changing American Borders and Identities

states, President Lincoln solidified the order by introducing the 13th Amendment, approved by the end of 1865, which states, "Neither slavery nor involuntary servitude, except as a punishment for crime whereof the party shall have been duly convicted, shall exist within the United States, or any place subject to their jurisdiction." This amendment directly helped free US slaves.

When the Civil War came to an end in 1865, between 620,000 to 850,000 American soldiers had died.[10] Like Native Americans and Mexican Americans, Black Americans continued to face discrimination and were often seen as inferior to whites, with a push from white Americans to "fit in" or assimilate.

President Abraham Lincoln signs the Emancipation Proclamation.

Examining Assimilation

The Great Wave of Immigration

From the 1850s through to the 1920s, the United States' population grew rapidly with an influx of immigrants from around the world. During the California Gold Rush of 1848–1854 and beyond, Chinese immigrants significantly contributed to the economic development of the West Coast through manual labor in agriculture, railroad construction, mining, and more. As white blue-collar workers feared losing their jobs to the Chinese immigrants who were paid much less, anti-Chinese sentiment, called sinophobia, grew steadily and led to the adoption of the Chinese Exclusion Act of 1882. This immigration law was the first of its kind and drastically reduced the arrival of more Chinese people and forbade Chinese immigrants who had already settled in the United States from becoming citizens until the law was repealed in 1943.[11]

In 1906, President Theodore Roosevelt introduced the Bureau of Immigration and Naturalization to establish a set of rules for foreign-born residents who were eligible for naturalization. Naturalization is the process where residents of a country become citizens. People born within the United States (or adopted by US citizens) are automatically granted citizenship, but people who arrive to the country after birth must seek naturalization. Citizenship is extremely important in the US because it means people can participate in our political system by voting or running for office, live in the country without fear of deportation, and have an active voice in conversations about the future of the country. Even as the United States' borders and laws changed, citizenship for

Changing American Borders and Identities

Chinese immigrants circa 1855 pan for gold in California.

Examining Assimilation

people of color was severely delayed and not always a right in spite of the Constitution.

The height of US immigration came in 1907 when approximately 1.3 million newcomers arrived. Known as the Great Wave of Immigration, the majority of new arrivals came from Europe and entered through New York's Ellis Island. On the West Coast, Angel Island in San Francisco Bay would serve as the main point of entry for immigrants from Asian countries a few decades later. By 1917, new immigrants

Pop Quiz: Immigration

Test your knowledge of immigration facts in the United States with this true or false quiz.

1. Over 43 million immigrants live in the United States.
2. Legal immigration is quick, easy, and affordable.
3. Most immigrants don't pay taxes.
4. Immigrants are less likely to commit violent crimes than US-born citizens.
5. Border walls are effective.

Answers: 1. True; **2.** False—Wait times vary from 6 to 25 years depending on circumstances. The line was about 4 million people long in 2013. Legal immigration can cost nearly $4,000 USD.; **3.** False—Immigrants pay taxes as regularly as US-born citizens. A 2007 governmental report estimated that up to 75 percent of undocumented immigrants even paid taxes. **4.** True. **5.** False—Research shows that border walls across the world don't prevent people from entering unlawfully. Rather they're costly symbols.

Changing American Borders and Identities

Immigrants arrive at Angel Island in the San Francisco Bay by sea circa 1911.

were required to pass medical examinations and literacy tests. When World War I broke out, immigration officers were expected to inspect incoming residents to prevent "enemies" from entering. As a result, the next period of immigration is remembered as an era of fear and mass restriction.

CHAPTER 3

Outlawing the Other

With the influx of immigrants in the United States came an influx of ideas for how newcomers should fit in with their new communities. Twenty-sixth president Theodore Roosevelt served two full terms until 1909. A speech he delivered on what it means to be American in 1915 reflects a way of thinking that was deeply popular in the United States at the time and has since carried on, though to a lesser extent.[1] Nativism is a strong preference for Americans born in the United States with an equally strong dislike and fear of immigrants said to have originated in the mid-nineteenth century. Nativists believe that white American Protestants should be the most important people to consider when making laws and that immigrants and people of color are not born with the same skills or abilities of white American Protestants.[2] Those beliefs, however, are not based in science and are xenophobic (hateful and fearful of strangers or people from other countries and their traditions) and prejudiced.

Nativism and the Age of Restriction

In his 1915 speech, Roosevelt said, "We should insist that if the immigrant who comes here in good faith becomes an American and assimilate himself to us, he shall be treated on exact equality with everyone else... Any man who says he is an American, but something else also, isn't an American at all. We have room for but one flag."[3] This speech is important to remember because it marks a time when immigrants, including those who are now considered white like Irish Americans and German Americans, were often expected to distance themselves from their home countries.

Outlawing the Other

When the United States government enacted the Immigration Act of 1924, the first law that limited the arrival of immigrants based solely on numbers, other laws that forced assimilation and penalized the "other" were already in place. While many immigrants choose to assimilate as a means of survival or to help their chances of succeeding within mainstream society, many people of color were not historically given the option and instead were deliberately stripped of culture and choice.

Indian Boarding Schools

Even though Native Americans had lived on the lands of the Americas for centuries, as soon as the borders changed they were expected to swiftly assimilate, or become "Americanized." Native people were called "savages" and considered "uncivilized" simply because their traditions, customs, and

Examining Assimilation

Seeking Refuge

Refugees are people who must leave their home countries to flee violence, persecution, and war. They move to other countries because they can't live safely anymore. In 1948, the US Congress approved the Displaced Persons Act that allowed refugees to resettle in the United States While the first wave of refugees were primarily from Europe, nearly 77 percent of refugees since 1975 are Indochinese or former citizens of the Soviet Union. The Refugee Act of 1980 was created to provide ongoing support for refugee resettlement. From 2001 through 2016, most refugees came to the United States from Burma (Myanmar), Iraq, Somalia, Bhutan, and Iran.

Refugee camps offer temporary settlement places for people who must flee their home country. Here, Bhutanese refugees eat lunch before leaving for the United States.

skin color were different from nativists who believed Americans born in the United States with European ancestry were naturally smarter and better. While the US government had spent decades fighting Native tribes with war and weapons, in 1868, a Montana congressman named James Michael Cavanaugh argued in favor of the proposed "Indian Appropriation Bill." During the debate, Cavanaugh said, "I have never in my life seen a good Indian except when I have seen a dead Indian." This quote is often shortened to "the only good Indian is a dead Indian" and was repeated many times throughout history as a way to justify what came next.[4] Rather than physically kill Native Americans again, the US government set out to kill their spirit, way of life, and, ultimately, their culture, because it was cheaper and more effective.[5]

Carlisle Indian Industrial School

In 1879, the first Indian boarding school was founded by military Captain Richard H. Pratt. Between 1879 and 1904, thousands of Native American children were taken from their homes and enrolled in Carlisle Indian Industrial School in Carlisle, Pennsylvania. Most students were kidnapped or coerced by the government with threats of withholding rations and clothing from families who refused to send their children. "Kill the Indian, save the man," was the philosophy of Carlisle Indian Industrial School as stated by Pratt.

Children were intentionally separated from their families, many miles away from home, and were forced to discard their Native American traditions. Students were punished

Examining Assimilation

WOUNDED YELLOW ROBE — HENRY STANDING BEAR — CHAUNCY YELLOW ROBE
SIOUX BOYS AS THEY ENTERED THE SCHOOL IN 1883. — THREE YEARS LATER.

Three students from the Sioux Nation are shown as they arrived at the Carlisle Indian Industrial School, and the same students were again photographed after three years at the school.

for practicing Native religions, using indigenous languages They wore American-style clothing in place of clothing from home. While Native American traditions encourage long hair for boys and men, young boys' hair was cut into short European styles. Teachers at these institutions considered their role to "civilize" or "Americanize" Native students rather than to teach. Children were abused, both physically and sexually. Years later, gravesites have been found where those who died were buried without notice. The peak of Indian boarding schools was in the 1970s and many were closed by the early 1990s.[6] Major changes have been made to the way the boarding schools for Native American students operate for those that remain open today. The earlier years especially, however, mark another period of intense trauma for Native Americans at the hands of the US government.

The English-Only Movement

In addition to governmental regulations aimed at making Native American youth give up their indigenous languages, nativist lawmakers also targeted other non-English languages across the country such as Spanish, German, Hawaiian, and Asian languages including Japanese, Chinese, and Korean. A strong anti-German attitude developed in the United States after World War I. Although German was widely studied in schools, most states dropped the language from their curriculums by 1922. Around the same time, the state of Nebraska made it illegal for people to speak non-English languages in public and the state of Iowa required schools to teach English only. Approximately 18,000 people were charged with violating English-only laws after these rulings. Some states even went as far to try to not teach students who spoke languages other than English at all, but these laws were overturned in court cases.[7] Even so, the majority of states created laws that specify English as the official language although the United States has never had an official language.

In 1920, it was also illegal to speak Hawaiian in schools and children who spoke the language faced physical punishment. A few years later, the Hawaiian territorial government introduced English Standard Schools. While the

Examining Assimilation

A famous cheesesteak eatery in Philadelphia sparked discrimination complaints with their "Speak English" signs in 2006. But in 2016, after the original owner passed away, the signs were removed.

schools' missions said they focused on English literacy, in reality they were addressing anxieties about "Oriental" influence and predominantly served white students. Students of color who did attend were segregated and discouraged from using non-English languages. Preserving aspects of culture, such as being proud to be Japanese, was interpreted as anti-American and was forbidden.[8]

Forced Out

Mexican American and Latinx communities faced similar struggles when it came to education, discrimination, and living peacefully. By the late 1920s, the Great Depression was in full effect and many Americans blamed immigrants for "stealing jobs." Although the US government never issued

Outlawing the Other

an official order, local and state governments across the country launched "repatriation" missions. "Repatriations" meant forced deportation.

In 1936, Colorado announced all "Mexicans" would have to leave the state, but this really meant anyone assumed to be of Latin American descent or who spoke Spanish. Colorado deported about eighty-two thousand people to Mexico and, by the end of the year, up to two million people were repatriated—approximately 60 percent of whom were US citizens. Latinx students were also expected to attend run-down, poorly funded "Mexican schools" until 1946 when Sylvia Mendez, an American-born Mexican Puerto Rican, and her family filed a lawsuit against the school district and won.[9] It would be a decade more until Black students were able to attend school alongside other races.

Japanese Internment

When the first major wave of Japanese immigrants arrived in Hawaii and on the West Coast, the anti-Chinese sentiments from the Gold Rush era were still strong and Chinese immigrants faced ongoing discrimination. Eventually, this expanded and became an overall anti-Asian sentiment. During World War II, Japanese immigrants and their American-born children became to be seen as security threats when the United States went to war with Japan. After the Japanese Navy bombed Pearl Harbor in Hawaii, the President Roosevelt issued Executive Order 9066 and jailed more than 100,000 people of Japanese ancestry, who mainly lived on the West Coast. The government forced people of

Examining Assimilation

From 1942 to 1945, approximately 100,000 Americans of Japanese descent had to leave their homes and live in internment camps.

Japanese descent to move to internment camps—many of whom were US citizens who were supposed to have the same rights as other Americans. Families were forced to stay for up to four years in these camps, away from their homes and communities, and with a significantly reduced quality of life.[10] Japanese Americans who had farms before the war had to sell their land and those who had family businesses had to close them suddenly. When internment ended, they returned to unfamiliar, changed places, and without many resources.

Outlawing the Other

The Jim Crow Era

Although the 13th Amendment was supposed to officially free enslaved Black Americans in 1865, racist lawmakers in the South created strict laws based on race to challenge the amendment immediately. These Black Codes, or "Jim Crow" laws, put limits on how Black citizens (aka "freed slaves") could work, earn, and live. The laws were a legal way to go around the 13th Amendment and created an environment where Black citizens couldn't vote or have a voice in the political system.[11] Because the Civil War was recent, the police officers and judges in the South were often ex-Confederate soldiers who had owned slaves. As a result, it

A segregated drinking fountain in the South.

39

Examining Assimilation

was very difficult for Black Americans to win court cases and very easy for them to face criminal charges. In prison, Black Americans were, again, treated like slaves.

As time went on, the Jim Crow laws expanded. Because the laws eventually restricted use of public areas and services by Blacks, much of daily life became separated. Buildings had separate, or segregated, entrances, elevators, water fountains, and more by law. Even living in white neighborhoods was forbidden for Black Americans. "Whites only" and "colored" signs were hung to inform people who could use what. By the 1920s, lynchings and violence against Black Americans had increased and Jim Crow laws appeared across the country. Even as Black Americans were supposed to be free and treated as equals, in practice they were not. A US Supreme Court ruling in 1954 called *Brown v. Board of Education* determined that segregation in school was unconstitutional and by 1964, in large part thanks to the efforts of activists during the civil rights movement, President Lyndon B. Johnson signed the Civil Rights Act into law. Another pair of laws, the Voting Rights Act of 1965 and Fair Housing Act of 1968, solidified the country's commitment to ending discrimination and legal racism.[12]

CHAPTER 4

Why We Assimilate

Today, there isn't one main view of assimilation or a single way to assimilate that's accepted by all. As assimilation takes many aspects of culture into consideration, it is very hard to study. Conversations about assimilation were once centered on the belief that it was a positive behavior. Previous generations that tried to achieve "full assimilation" or encouraged it didn't really clarify what that meant. It was generally seen as something desirable and achievable by immigrants and refugees, but it wasn't consistently defined. Today, it's unclear if "full assimilation" is possible for people of color, although ethnic groups like Italians and Poles are now considered white and fully assimilated. Assimilation isn't simply good or bad, but being forced to behave in new ways because your lifestyle is considered "less than" isn't okay. There are many valid reasons why people choose to assimilate or not. Assimilation, like the United States, is complex.

Examining Assimilation

Why Assimilate?

Families, like society, are big influences for people and both often encourage assimilation. For many people, assimilation has been a key for survival and it has opened up certain opportunities that wouldn't have been available otherwise. Before their internment, for example, Japanese immigrants and their families often led very intentional lifestyles influenced by traditional Japanese culture and customs.[1] From the foods they ate to how much value they placed on friendship and exercise, many customs carried on from Japanese upbringings. Following their internment, however, becoming "more American" was necessary to live.

Issei, which refers to the Japanese immigrants who came to the United States and were ineligible for citizenship until 1952, raised their children, the Nisei, who were often the first generation of Japanese Americans born in the country.[2] Since the Issei had lived through painful decades of intense discrimination and a loss of rights due to their ethnicity, adopting American values and culturally assimilating was encouraged to Nisei as protection and prevention of further discrimination. Nisei were given names that were "more American" like Kevin and Linda, weren't taught to speak Japanese, and were pressed to pursue education and financial success. Less than twenty years after the internment, Japanese Americans were high economic and academic achievers, often used as an example by society to highlight the best outcomes of assimilation. This frequent praise earned them the stereotype of being the "model minority," but for many Asian Americans this meant added pressure to assimilate

Why We Assimilate

and excel. Even in 2000, journalist Annie Nakao said, "Today, Japanese Americans are the very symbol of assimilation—upwardly mobile, marrying outside their ethnic group at high rates, and dispersing throughout suburban America."[3]

In their 2016 book, *The Myth of the Model Minority: Asian Americans Facing Racism*, authors Rosalind S. Chou and Joe R. Feagin interview many Asian Americans to share their diverse experiences of assimilation and race. A man named Brian tells the authors about being raised by an Issei who had been interned during WWII: "[Assimilation] was reinforced

The model minority myth can add pressure onto students of Asian descent while ignoring ethnic disparities and struggles.

Examining Assimilation

from the rest of the [Japanese] culture, but there was also a strong [household] push for us to assimilate, to [be] raised to conformist status, and to be as white in America as possible." Brian's father saw assimilation as a necessary path to opportunity.

Passing as White

For African Americans living during the Jim Crow era, assimilation was available only to those with fair skin. Rather than having the ability to be "model minorities," the only option for Black people with fair skin was to try to "pass," or be seen, as a white person. Being seen as white meant they could vote, have safety and rights, work in offices, have access to everything previously unavailable for Black people during segregation, and ultimately have a chance to live more equal lives. Families would encourage passing when the option was available. Since many parents want to help their children succeed, be safe, and live as freely as possible, many examples can be found of older generations across cultures in the United States encouraging assimilation out of love for their children.

Religious Assimilation

While language is a key element of assimilation, culture goes far beyond language. Some aspects of culture are physical or material, like architecture, clothing, art, technology, and cars. But much of what cultural assimilation focuses on are nonmaterial ideas like social habits, beliefs, and values.

While the US Constitution and early American society strongly believed in Protestant Christianity as the only suitable religion, the country has become more religiously diverse over time. About 70 percent of people in the United States report practicing Christianity (including branches like Protestant, Catholic, etc.) as of 2017, while Judaism makes up about 2 percent and Islam, Buddhism, and Hinduism are each approximately 1 percent of the population. Religiously unaffiliated, atheist, or agnostic make up 22 percent.[4]

Like other areas of cultural assimilation, religious minorities are more likely to face discrimination and prejudice based on their religion. In recent years, Muslim and Sikh communities have experienced a large increase in intolerance and aggression—first after the terror attacks of September 11, 2001 (9/11) in the United States and again after the 2016 US presidential election.[5] Muslims are people who practice Islam—the second largest religion in the world—while Sikhs practice Sikhism.[6] Although they are very different religions, some people who are unfamiliar or unaware of the religions confuse them. Both religions call for their followers to wear specific clothing and accessories as a way of showing their devotion, but they often face discrimination because of hurtful and negative stereotypes associated with what they wear.

After Islamist extremist group al-Qaeda carried out the 9/11 attacks, there was a large increase in reports of physical attacks against Muslims in the United States, jumping from twelve reports in 2000 to 93 in 2001. Over the years, that number had mostly dropped, but following the 2016

Examining Assimilation

People from many religious congregations gather during the inaugural Queens Interfaith Unity Walk in New York in 2009.

presidential election, 127 reports of anti-Muslim assault were filed in 2016.[7] For Muslims and Sikhs, following cultural assimilation by abandoning traditional dress (like hijabs and turbans) would mean rejecting their religion. While it may likely mean more safety and less discrimination in the United States, a belief in God usually comes first.

Other examples of religious dress include kippahs or yarmulkes for Jewish men, bonnets worn by Amish or Mennonite women, and veils for Catholic nuns. However, like Muslims and Sikhs, Jews have also faced an increase in recent harassment because of their religion. While physical assaults were down in 2017, anti-Semitism (prejudice against Jews) in the form of the vandalism, bomb threats, and threats at school

Why We Assimilate

Who Is Jazz Jennings?

Jazz Jennings knew she was a girl since she could speak. Although she was assigned male at birth in 2000, she decided to live life as a girl when she was just five years old with her family's support. Today, Jazz is one of the world's youngest transgender figures and activists.

The Jewish teen has written a children's picture book and memoir about her life. Jazz is the reality TV star of *I am Jazz*, which premiered in 2015. Although it can be hard to live so publicly, she told *People* in 2017, "Someone has to do it to get the education out there. A lot of people are kind of ignorant to transgender issues and it's important that we share our stories in order to change those minds and open peoples' hearts."

Learn more about Jazz on YouTube (JazzMergirl) and Instagram (@jazzjennings_)

were significantly up. Even as anti-Semitism continues to be reported less around the world in forty countries, the United States, Australia, and Britain show the opposite trends.[8]

LGBTQ Culture

LGBTQ is an acronym used to cover a spectrum of sexualities and identities besides heterosexuality (aka "straight") that includes lesbian, gay, bisexual, trans, queer, intersex,

Examining Assimilation

nonbinary, and more. Larger conversations around cultural assimilation often exclude the LGBTQ community, but assimilation, first and foremost, is a push for subordinate or minority groups to blend in, which definitely includes gender and sexuality.

LGBTQ people, like heterosexual people, have existed since ancient times and varying public attitudes have coincided.[9] For centuries, being LGBTQ was misunderstood as a sinful lifestyle choice even though it has been scientifically proven to be genetic (something people are born with.)[10] As being LGBTQ isn't something a person can choose to be, certain activities won't "cause" anyone to be LGBTQ. Homosexuality in particular was once considered a mental disorder from 1968 to 1973 by the American Psychiatric Association and was classified as a disease by the World Health Organization until it was removed in 1992.[11] Meanwhile, Two Spirit identities in Native American culture have long embraced gender as a spectrum with many expressions, and various countries and cultures around the world are more accepting and understanding of LGBTQ people.[12]

LGBTQ people frequently experience stigma and prejudice today, even though there have been many historical achievements toward acceptance and progress. Like other minority groups, assimilating can provide protection for LBGTQ people from violence, bullying, and harassment, but it often means hiding aspects of their identity and true self.

Some ways that an LGBTQ person might assimilate include keeping their gender identity and/or sexuality secret out of fear or uncertainty, choosing not to correct

Why We Assimilate

Trans women of color activists Sylvia Rivera and Marsha P. Johnson were at the forefront of the Stonewall Riots of 1969, which sparked momentum for the first Pride parade the next year.

people for using incorrect pronouns (ex. he, she, they,) and dressing or behaving according to traditional Western gender roles even if it doesn't feel natural. According to a study by RTI International, "LGBTQ+ persons experience violence and victimization in disproportionate numbers throughout childhood, adolescence, and adulthood. Despite the perception that society is becoming more open and welcoming of LGBTQ+ persons, victimization disparities have not improved since the 1990s."[13] Therefore, respecting LGBTQ people and their identities is essential to creating a society that is accepting of all people and to celebrate diversity in every form.

CHAPTER 5

A Culture of Assimilation

Since cultural assimilation is deeply engrained in our society, it can be hard to see the ways it affects our lives every day. Even today, the centuries old origins of cultural assimilation are visible. In some ways, assimilation has become part of US culture itself, but that doesn't always mean it should be accepted or preserved. From calling school lunches stinky to adopting "American names" and changing the way we speak, schools, peers, families, and different social environments continue to encourage assimilation today.

Looking at the Media Lens

Mass media is a form of communication that informs people about the world we live in. If you've ever watched TV, browsed a magazine, liked a meme on Instagram, or listened to the radio, you've consumed media in some form. As technology has advanced, so has the definition

A Culture of Assimilation

Food shaming in the school cafeteria is a common experience, especially for students from immigrant families.

of media, which now includes "amateur" material like blogs and social media. Even as the definition and forms of media change, its immense influence remains the same.

Whether in written, visual, or audio form, every piece of media has a purpose. Sometimes the purpose is to educate and inform people, like with the news, and other times it is meant purely for entertainment. Advertisements, another form of media, convince people to buy things. But what does media have to do with cultural assimilation? Media spreads ideas and attitudes that can change the way we think, behave, and see other cultures as well as our own.

Examining Assimilation

In the United States, newsrooms continue to primarily employ white male journalists. Over the past two decades, the percentage of people of color in the newsrooms across the country has stayed about the same with the Pew Research Center reporting twelve percent of all newsroom staff in 2012.[1] Latinx, Black, and Asian women journalists account for less than five percent of newsroom staff as of 2016.[2] As news outlets are supposed to cover all of society's topics and issues, homogeneity (being the same) in the newsroom often means only one perspective is shared. The same lack of diversity and homogeneity is present in Hollywood and the entertainment industry as well.[3] And since media is mainly run by white men, a Eurocentric viewpoint is the perspective most often seen.

People of color and women are underrepresented in the media and their stories tend to be told using stereotypes

For an interactive look at US newsroom diversity in 2017, visit goo.gl/trends/asne.

A Culture of Assimilation

when portrayed.[4] Stereotypes are overly simplified depictions and assumptions of people based on their identities (race, gender, sexuality, etc.) that are often negative. Some common racial and ethnic stereotypes in the news include portraying Muslims as terrorists, Blacks as thugs, Native Americans as alcoholics, Asians as overly frugal, and Latinxs as lazy, undocumented immigrants.[5] In films and television, people from minority groups are often depicted using stereotypes, tropes (clichés), and one-dimensional storylines, like in news stories. Many of the racist stereotypes we think of today originate from deliberate media and ad campaigns in the past that wanted to create fear and reinforce certain cultures as inferior.

Since every form of media is shared for a reason, it's important to be able to analyze and identify the messages behind media and consider who created it, what prejudices they may have, and what effects media makers expect or anticipate. Historically, media has intentionally promoted racist beliefs, fear of others, and cultural assimilation. Current research shows that media coverage often negatively influences peoples' perceptions of immigrants. All forms of media, including social media, typically reinforce stereotypes as well.[6]

Assimilation at School

Schools, like the media, affect the way we see one another and understand the world. Students naturally feel a strong desire to fit in and belong, but young people often experience bullying in school because of their differences. Education

Examining Assimilation

is one of the most effective ways to teach acceptance and to debunk the myths and stereotypes we may learn from media, other peers, and our families. Teachers, standardized test authors, and the historians who typically write textbooks are predominantly white and this means we learn from a Eurocentric perspective that often minimizes the painful realities of our past and even intentionally misrepresents people of color by relying on racist stereotypes.[7]

A classic example is the untrue history of Thanksgiving Day, which Abraham Lincoln even made a national holiday as an attempt to unify the American people during the Civil War.[8] Another way we can see Eurocentricity is by the lack of equal representation for prominent figures who are people of color or LGBTQ, even though there have been plenty throughout history. When marginalized people are depicted in textbooks, painful and traumatic stories are most often told.

Beyond erasure in history, students often self-segregate by race or ethnicity and reinforce the idea that there's only one way to be. In the cafeteria, students who don't bring bologna on white bread are teased for enjoying lunches of kimchi fried rice or palaak paneer. On the flip side, phrases like coconut, Oreo, banana, and apple are used to accuse peers of not being "ethnic" enough and "whitewashed." Stereotypes even carry into the classroom and can affect which students are seen as inherently smart, even though students and people of every race are smart and capable of high achievement and success when given equal opportunity.

LGBTQ students are twice as likely as their peers to have been physically assaulted at school and 42 percent report

A Culture of Assimilation

not feeling accepted in the community where they live. A significant majority also say they hear negative messages about being LGBTQ from their school, classmates, and the internet.[9] At the same time, LGBTQ youth can feel excluded and unsafe, and face discrimination in places like gym locker rooms, bathrooms, school dances, and gendered activities like Girl Scouts.[10]

Another way students can feel discouraged from being perceived as "different" is through speech and names. Although every person has an accent of some kind, many Americans think of the "ideal accent" and a neutral accent as Midwestern.[11] People in the past and present often

As many as one in three students report facing bullying at school. Bullying is serious and can lead to feelings of isolation, depression, anxiety, and even suicidal thoughts that may last into adulthood.

Examining Assimilation

mistake accents and dialects as a marker of intelligence and stigmatize people who speak "with accents" or those who don't speak "proper" English. These ideas go beyond schools and into the workplace as well.

African American Vernacular English (AAVE) is a dialect that categorizes the manner in which some Black people speak. You can find examples of AAVE throughout pop culture from television to the majority of successful memes. Although phrases may originate within AAVE, white people and non-Black people of color often use these terms, especially on the internet, to sound funny and clever. But even as words like "salty," "shade," "shook," and "bae" become standard words in many peoples' vocabularies, it's still seen as improper and unprofessional in school and work settings—especially when used by Black people.

Black students who choose to wear their hair in natural styles or opt for head wraps or dreads may face teasing and discrimination from peers and authority figures alike. Similarly, students who choose to wear hijabs or don't conform to expectations of dress according to gender may feel excluded and bullied. More subtly, students can reinforce Eurocentric beauty standards by teasing others for having body hair, dark skin, or single eyelids.

Finally, students who have names that aren't stereotypically "American" may end up receiving unwanted nicknames, hearing their name regularly mispronounced or forgotten, and may even adopt new names altogether. When teachers and students don't make a point of learning how to

A Culture of Assimilation

Headwraps originated in sub-Saharan Africa. In addition to serving as a beauty statement, headwraps offer hair protection and symbolize spirituality and tradition depending on the culture.

pronounce someone's name, it's hurtful and can make people of any background feel like they don't belong.

Bringing Assimilation Home

Families play a major influence in how we relate to and treat others. At home, cultural assimilation may or may not be an explicit topic of conversation, but it can be practiced in different ways and affect our lives to varying levels. As illustrated by Vy H`ông Phạm's story, naming traditions may change, especially the longer that families and their children are in their new country. Although Latin American families

Examining Assimilation

New School, New Name

When Vy H`ông Phạm and her family arrived in the United States as refugees from Vietnam in 1991, they moved into a thriving Vietnamese Catholic community in Hartford, Connecticut. After several years, Vy's parents decided to move to a nearby town where, at her new school, Vy was the only Asian student in the third grade. To avoid mispronunciation and teasing, Vy legally changed her name to Christina.

She says she doesn't regret changing her name because it was a survival tactic but is sad that she had to alter her identity. Almost two decades later, she chose to reclaim her birth name and goes by Vy to friends and family. "It felt like the right thing to do," she says. "I aligned the way I see myself with how I want the external world to see me."

commonly use two last names (one from each parent), it's common to only use one surname in the United States. Many governmental databases are even unable to add two last names, and so people with two last names must pick one, even if they don't necessarily want to.

Although immigrants and refugees are often accused of refusing to speak English due to "laziness," basic English proficiency is part of the legal immigration process, and a book on language, education, and immigration found that "most immigrants lose their ancestral language within two to three generations."[12] Immigrant parents may delay or forgo speaking to their children in their native languages as

A Culture of Assimilation

As of 2015, at least 350 different languages are spoken in homes across the United States.

a way to eliminate the likelihood of having difficulty with pronunciation and to prevent teasing. On the other side, English language learners may stop speaking in their native language as children to "blend in."

Since cultural assimilation is, in many ways, rooted in the belief that one way of life is better than others, communities that are especially pressured to assimilate may begin to accept this idea as truth.

Internalization

Sociology is the scientific study of society and psychology is the scientific study of human behavior and minds. Cultural

Examining Assimilation

assimilation is often discussed in terms of sociology, but a key element of "successful" cultural assimilation is actually internalization, or the point where the people who are pressured to assimilate believe that it is the only way to succeed and that others, including them, who don't are less than. Internalization is usually unconscious, or something that feels like it naturally happens and isn't a decision that is thought about.

At home and in public, this might mean children of immigrants start to correct their parents for speaking "bad

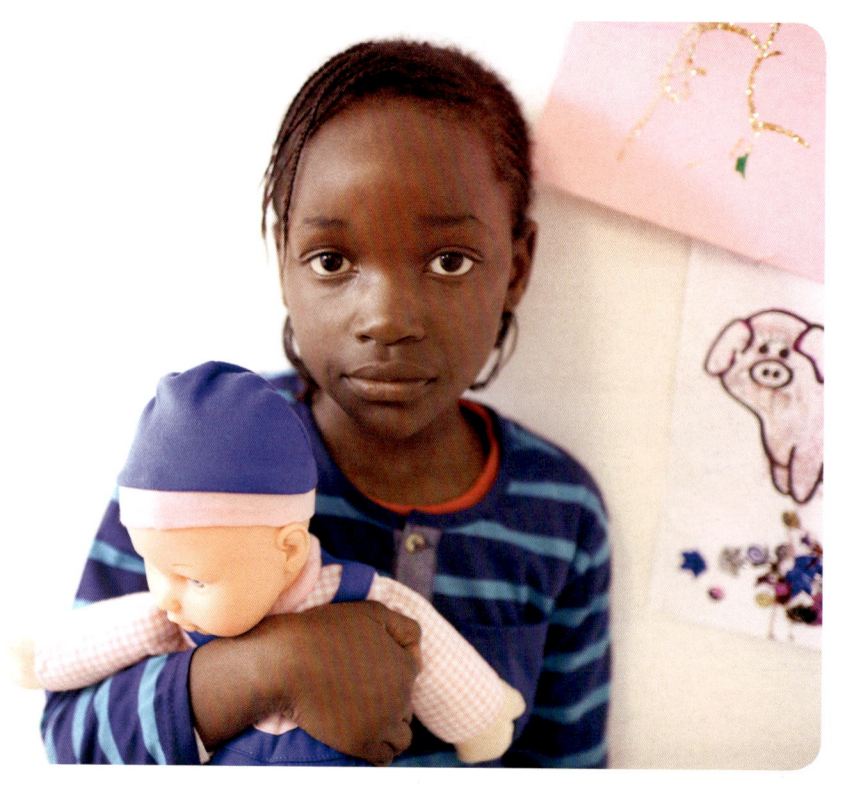

External influences, such as a lack of diverse and culturally representative dolls and toys, can contribute to internalization.

A Culture of Assimilation

English" in an unkind way or may separate themselves from peers who don't fit in with the ideal "American identity." Students may choose to go by "Robert" instead of "Roberto," for example, and say it sounds better without realizing they're showing a preference for white American names. Furthermore, students may diet, pluck their eyebrows, straighten their hair with a flat iron or relaxer, and wear colored contacts as another way to better fit in with the Eurocentric beauty ideals our society has taught people to value more. Even though internalization can be hard to see, when people self-reflect on their behaviors and thoughts, they can start to see the ways they conform, or go along, with society's expectations of them rather than following their hearts or what they want. Internalization, like racism and prejudice, is a learned behavior, so it can be unlearned with practice, education, and intention.

CHAPTER 6

How to Combat Assimilation

Today, US society continues to debate the relevancy of cultural assimilation. The idea that immigrants all blend in and lose their cultural identities, like the melting pot metaphor, is becoming less popular.[1] Instead, cultural *acculturation* is sometimes proposed as an alternative to assimilation that doesn't require a loss of cultural identity.

Acculturation over Assimilation?

Acculturation is the idea that immigrants and refugees accept the culture of their new countries while "retaining the traditions of their original heritage."[2] Acculturation is a mutual exchange which means that both sides—immigrants and the dominant groups—share parts of their culture with one another and integrate all cultures. For example, cuisine in the United States is a good example of what acculturation can look like. Just as a family may enjoy burgers and chow mein at home,

How to Combat Assimilation

greater society may enjoy dim sum, hot dogs, and fried chicken. Clothing, music, slang, language, and holidays are other examples of potential exchange via acculturation. Latinx people and white people may attend quinceañeras and sweet sixteen celebrations alike. Musical fusions may emerge such as Cambodian psychedelic rock and the incorporation of bhangra beats into hip hop. Even as many communities speak English in the United States, Yiddish, a language used by Ashkenazi Jews before the Holocaust, is another example of mutual exchange. Today, words like "schlep" for haul, "schmooze" for small talk, and "klutz" for clumsy people are commonly used by non-native Yiddish speakers with ease.

A family breaks fast (called iftar) during Ramadan, a sacred month-long Muslim holiday.

Examining Assimilation

On a personal level, however, acculturation means that people change the way they live their lives. This may sound like assimilation, the key difference is that acculturation allows room for viewing both native and new cultures as important and worthy. Individually, people can see themselves as equals, even if all of society doesn't yet and even if people from minority groups continue to be marginalized and overlooked by society in favor of the dominant culture (as is the case in the United States). Some people may view themselves as bicultural, living and embodying two or more cultures, while others may see their identities as a third culture, blended of new and old.

Reclaiming Culture

For youth and adults who decide to embrace culture, it can be hard to know how to regain a sense of culture if aspects have already been lost. Sometimes culture has been shed by the individual person, and other times, their families have made the decision to shed their culture in a previous generation. It can be stressful and confusing for people who feel like their cultural identities are at odds with the majority culture. They may have to figure out how to live with authenticity and individuality, but there are many ways to explore cultural identity.

One of the best ways to learn about yourself is to learn about your culture. Asking parents and older relatives about family history can provide a deeper understanding of the stories that helped shape future generations. Food and holidays are excellent ways to reconnect with culture

How to Combat Assimilation

and ancestry. Even if family members may not have recipes to pass down, there are amazing cookbooks that offer history and traditional recipes according to culture like *The Sioux Chef's Indigenous Kitchen* by Sean Sherman, *Decolonize Your Diet* by Luz Calvo and Catriona Rueda Esuqibel, *The Jemima Code: Two Centuries of African American Cookbooks* by Toni Tipton-Martin, and *The Cooking Gene* by Michael W. Twitty.

If learning the language of a native country or heritage is important, students can enroll in classes online and in person, use apps and computer programs like DuoLingo, and practice with relatives or language groups that know the language or are also learning. Watching TV shows, listening

Grandparents and older family members can share memories and stories you may not remember or that happened before you were born!

Examining Assimilation

to podcasts, and reading books in other languages greatly helps with developing the skills for that language.

Choosing to consume media that does represent your culture respectfully and vividly is another way to honor and explore your identity. Sitcoms like *Blackish*, *Fresh Off the Boat*, *Jane the Virgin*, and *The Mindy Project* are examples of recent or current shows that portray people of color well beyond stereotypes. Code-switching—the practice of alternating between different dialects or languages depending on setting—is another common way that people choose to acculturate and maintain aspects of their culture they value while following societal expectations.

Jane the Virgin *celebrates the splendor of telenovelas, or Latin American soap operas, through the story of Jane Villanueva and her family.*

How to Combat Assimilation

The Magic of Melanin

Melanin is the pigmentation, or coloring, that determines people's skin color. There are different types of melanin, which can also be found in hair, pupils, and eyes.[3] Melanin protects skin against the sun's UV rays and is a natural form of sunblock, although people of all shades should use sunblock products for sufficient protection. People in warmer climates tend to have darker skin than people who live in colder climates. As melanin shields the skin from harmful sun rays, however, people with darker complexions absorb vitamin D more slowly than people with light complexions, so having a diet rich in vitamin D helps keep these levels healthy.[4]

Ultimately, reclamation is about being proud of your cultural roots and celebrating the things that make people unique and beautiful. While it might take some time to unlearn negative ideas and the internalization that comes with a culture of assimilation, it's definitely possible!

Talking About Culture with Others

Sometimes, you may encounter people who are unfamiliar with your culture, just as you may come across people from cultures other than your own as well. You don't have a responsibility to teach other people about your culture, especially when someone approaches the subject with aggression or insensitivity. But, you can choose to talk about your culture when you want.

Examining Assimilation

For example, if someone asks where you are from or "What are you," you don't have to explain yourself to them. You can choose to be as specific or vague as you'd like, just as you have the power to do when people ask about any other topic in your life. If you choose to answer something broad like "California," you can remain firm in that answer, even if people may try to pressure you into giving a different answer. If people ask if you are of a specific minority group whether ethnic, religious, or in regard to sexuality, you can simply answer no, or yes, or say, "I don't feel comfortable discussing this." Likewise, if someone asks about the significance of a hijab or passes judgment on your beliefs or appearance, you

Everyone has a unique story and can learn to navigate culture and identity on their own terms.

don't have to talk to them. Finally, if a stranger asks if they can touch your hair, you can tell them no.

Resisting Limits and Embracing Change

While our many cultures and identities are important, they should never be used as an excuse to set limitations or expectations. People of all races, gender, sexuality, and ability are capable of being the lead in a school play and, similarly, all students can excel in academics and sports. Being a mixed race, multiracial, or transracial adoptee doesn't make you more or less a part of any culture.

As you continue to learn more about yourself and the world around you, it's important to remember that it's okay to change. While you may have once identified as "Hispanic," you may find that "Chicanx" is now more suitable. You won't know all the answers all the time, whether in regard to your culture or feelings, but no one does. Most importantly, remember your personal happiness is what matters and you're in control of your story, identity, and life.

Chapter Notes

Chapter 1
What Is Assimilation?

1. "QuickFacts," Census.gov, July 1, 2017, http://www.census.gov/quickfacts.
2. US Census Bureau, "New Census Bureau Report Analyzes US Population Projections," US Census Bureau, March 3, 2015, https://www.census.gov/newsroom/press-releases/2015/cb15-tps16.html.
3. Jason DeParle, "Favoring Immigration If Not the Immigrant," *New York Times*, May 8, 2011, http://www.nytimes.com/2011/05/09/books/a-nation-of-immigrants-susan-f-martins-book.html.
4. "Leif Eriksson," History.com, 2010, https://www.history.com/topics/exploration/leif-eriksson.
5. Amanda Briney, "A Brief History of the Age of Exploration," ThoughtCo., August 19, 2017, https://www.thoughtco.com/age-of-exploration-1435006.
6. Alfred W. Crosby, "The Columbian Exchange: Plants, Animals, and Disease between the Old and New Worlds," National Humanities Center, http://nationalhumanitiescenter.org/tserve/nattrans/ntecoindian/essays/columbianc.htm (accessed March 2018).
7. Alan Rice, "The Economic Basis of the Slave Trade," Revealing Histories, http://revealinghistories.org.uk/africa-the-arrival-of-europeans-and-the-transatlantic-slave-trade/articles/the-economic-basis-of-the-slave-trade.html (accessed March 2018).
8. Brendan Wolfe, "Slavery by the Numbers," *Encyclopedia Virginia*, December 1, 2011, https://www.evblog.virginiahumanities.org/2011/12/slavery-by-the-numbers/.
9. Christopher Woolf, "How the French Won the American Revolution," *PRI's The World,* July 4, 2014, https://www.pri.org/stories/2014-07-04/how-french-won-american-revolution.

Chapter 2
Changing American Borders and Identities

1. "Louisiana Purchase, 1803," History.state.gov, https://history.state.gov/milestones/1801-1829/louisiana-purchase (accessed March 2018).
2. "Indian Removal Act," The Library of Congress, March 27, 2018, https://www.loc.gov/rr/program/bib/ourdocs/Indian.html.

Chapter Notes

3. "Trail of Tears," History.com, 2009, https://www.history.com/topics/native-american-history/trail-of-tears.
4. Murray Lee, "What Is Tribal Sovereignty," Partnership with Native Americans, September 9, 2014, http://blog.nativepartnership.org/what-is-tribal-sovereignty/.
5. "Manifest Destiny and Indian Removal," Smithsonian American Art Museum, February 2015, http:/ /wp-content/uploads/2015/02/Manifest-Destiny-and-Indian-Removal.pdf.
6. Martha Menchaca, *Recovering History, Constructing Race: The Indian, Black, and White Roots of Mexican Americans* (Austin, TX: University of Texas Press, 2001), pp. 215–276.
7. Peter Nabokov, "Indians, Slaves, and Mass Murder: The Hidden History," *New York Review of Books,* November 24, 2016, http://www.nybooks.com/articles/2016/11/24/indians-slaves-and-mass-murder-the-hidden-history/.
8. Richard Griswold del Castill, "War's End: Treaty of Guadalupe Hidalgo," Pbs.org, http://www.pbs.org/kera/usmexicanwar/war/wars_end_guadalupe.html (accessed March 2018).
9. "Abraham Lincoln Papers at the Library of Congress," The Library of Congress, https://www.loc.gov/teachers/classroommaterials/connections/abraham-lincoln-papers/thinking3.html (accessed March 2018).
10. "Quick Facts: Civil War Facts," Civilwar.org, https://www.civilwar.org/learn/articles/civil-war-facts (accessed March 2018).
11. "Repeal of the Chinese Exclusion Act, 1943," History.state.gov, https://history.state.gov/milestones/1937-1945/chinese-exclusion-act-repeal (accessed March 2018).

Chapter 3
Outlawing the Other

1. "Nativism in America," United States History for Kids, July 1, 2014, http://www.american-historama.org/1881-1913-maturation-era/nativism-in-america.htm.

Examining Assimilation

2. Uri Friedman, "What Is a Nativist," *The Atlantic*, April 11, 2017, https://www.theatlantic.com/international/archive/2017/04/what-is-nativist-trump/521355/.
3. Julia Higgins, "The Rise and Fall of the American 'Melting Pot,'" *Wilson Quarterly*, December 5, 2015, https://wilsonquarterly.com/stories/the-rise-and-fall-of-the-american-melting-pot/.
4. Wolfgang Mieder, "'The Only Good Indian Is a Dead Indian': History and Meaning of a Proverbial Stereotype., *The Journal of American Folklore*, vol. 106, no. 419 (1993): pp. 38–60, JSTOR, www.jstor.org/stable/541345.
5. Toney Booth Tabath, "Cheaper Than Bullets: American Indian Boarding Schools and Assimilation Policy, 1890-1930," University of Central Oklahoma, http://www.se.edu/nas/files/2013/03/NAS-2009-Proceedings-Booth.pdf (accessed March 2018).
6. "American Indian Boarding Schools Haunt Many," NPR, May 12, 2008, https://www.npr.org/templates/story/story.php?storyId=16516865.
7. Denis Baron, "Official American: English Only," *Do You Speak American?*, 2005, http://www.pbs.org/speak/seatosea/officialamerican/englishonly/.
8. Morris Young, "Standard English and Student Bodies: Institutionalizing Racism and Literacy in Hawai'i," *College English,* vol. 64, no. 4 (2002): pp. 405–431, JSTOR, www.jstor.org/stable/3250745.
9. Caitlin Yoshiko Kandil, "Mendez vs. Segregation: 70 Years Later, Famed Case 'Isn't Just About Mexicans. It's About Everybody Coming Together,'" *Los Angeles Times*, April 17, 2016, http://www.latimes.com/socal/weekend/news/tn-wknd-et-0417-sylvia-mendez-70-anniversary-20160417-story.html.
10. Bill Ong Hing, "A Nation of Immigrants, a History of Nativism," *To Be an American: Cultural Pluralism and the Rhetoric of Assimilation* (New York, NY: NYU Press, 1997), pp. 13–31.
11. "Jim Crow Laws," History.com, 2018, https://www.history.com/topics/jim-crow-laws.
12. "Black Codes," History.com, 2010, https://www.history.com/topics/black-history/black-codes.

Chapter Notes

Chapter 4
Why We Assimilate

1. Joe Feagin and Rosalind Chou, *The Myth of the Model Minority: Asian Americans Facing Racism* (New York, NY: Routledge, 2016), pp. 1–56.
2. Lynn Jones, "Japanese American Immigration and Assimilation," Humboldt State University, 2005, http://humboldt-dspace.calstate.edu/bitstream/handle/2148/15/jones.pdf?sequence=3.
3. Annie Nakao, "Homing in on Japan," *SFGate*, September 10, 2000, https://www.sfgate.com/g00/news/article/Homing-in-on-Japan-3051471.php?i10c.encReferrer=aHR0cHM6Ly93d3cuZ29vZ2xlLmNvbS8%3D&i10c.ua=1&i10c.dv=13.
4. "Religious Landscape Study," Pew Research Center, http://www.pewforum.org/religious-landscape-study/ (accessed March 2018).
5. "Defending the Rights of Religious Minorities," ACLU.org, https://www.aclu.org/issues/religious-liberty/free-exercise-religion/defending-rights-religious-minorities (accessed March 2018).
6. "Largest Religions in the World," WorldAtlas.com, https://www.worldatlas.com/articles/largest-religions-in-the-world.html (accessed March 2018).
7. Katayoun Kishi, "Assaults Against Muslims in US Surpass 2001 Level," Pew Research Center, November 15, 2017, http://www.pewresearch.org/fact-tank/2017/11/15/assaults-against-muslims-in-u-s-surpass-2001-level/.
8. Jaweed Kaleem, "Anti-Semitism in US Surged in 2017, a New Report Finds," *Los Angeles Times*, February 26, 2018, http://www.latimes.com/nation/la-na-anti-semitism-adl-20180226-story.html.
9. Louis Crompton, *Homosexuality and Civilization* (Cambridge, MA: Harvard University Press, 2006), pp. 1–31.
10. Debra Soh, "Cross-Cultural Evidence for the Genetics of Homosexuality," *Scientific American*, April 25, 2017, https://www.scientificamerican.com/article/cross-cultural-evidence-for-the-genetics-of-homosexuality/.
11. Neel Burton, "When Homosexuality Stopped Being a Mental Disorder," *Psychology Today*, September 18, 2015, https://www.psychologytoday.com/us/blog/hide-and-seek/201509/when-homosexuality-stopped-being-mental-disorder.

Examining Assimilation

12. Tony Enos, "8 Things You Should Know About Two Spirit People," *Indian Country Today*, March 28, 2017, https://indiancountrymedianetwork.com/culture/social-issues/8-misconceptions-things-know-two-spirit-people/#.
13. Tasseli McKay, Shilpi Misra, and Christine Linquist, "Violence and LBGTQ+ Communities," RTI International, March 2017, https://www.rti.org/sites/default/files/rti_violence_and_lgbtq_communities.pdf.

Chapter 5
A Culture of Assimilation

1. Emily Guskin, "5 Facts About Ethnic and Gender Diversity in US Newsrooms," Pew Research Center, July 18, 2013, http://www.pewresearch.org/fact-tank/2013/07/18/5-facts-about-ethnic-and-gender-diversity-in-u-s-newsrooms/.
2. "2016 ASNE Diversity Study," ASNE.org, http://asne.org/files/Updated%20ASNE%20Diversity%20Survey%20Methodology%20and%20Tables.pdf (accessed March 2018).
3. Gordon Cox, "Hollywood Diversity and Inclusion See Little Rise in 10 Years (Study)," *Variety*, July 31, 2017, http://variety.com/2017/film/news/hollywood-diversity-little-rise-study-1202510809/.
4. Eric Deggans, "Researchers Examine Hollywood's Lack of Diversity," NPR, February 22, 2016, https://www.npr.org/2016/02/22/467621632/researchers-examine-hollywoods-lack-of-diversity.
5. Angie Chuang and Robin Chin Roemer, "Beyond the Positive–Negative Paradigm of Latino/Latina News-Media Representations: DREAM Act Exemplars, Stereotypical Selection, and American Otherness," *Journalism*, vol. 16, no. 8 (2015), https://doi.org/10.1177/1464884914550974.
6. Kaitlin Felsted, "How Social Media Affect the Social Identity of Mexican Americans," Brigham Young University, 2013, https://scholarsarchive.byu.edu/etd/3828.
7. Liana Loewus, "The Nation's Teaching Force Is Still Mostly White and Female," *Education Week*, March 26, 2018, https://www.edweek.org/ew/articles/2017/08/15/the-nations-teaching-force-is-still-mostly.html.

Chapter Notes

8. Gale Courey Toensing, "What Really Happened at the First Thanksgiving? The Wampanoag Side of the Tale," *Indian Country Today*, November 23, 2017, https://indiancountrymedianetwork.com/history/events/what-really-happened-at-the-first-thanksgiving-the-wampanoag-side-of-the-tale/.
9. "Growing Up LGBT in America," HRC.org, https://www.hrc.org/youth-report/view-and-share-statistics (accessed March 2018).
10. "Discrimination Against LGBT Youth in US Schools," HRW.org, https://www.hrw.org/report/2016/12/07/walking-through-hailstorm/discrimination-against-lgbt-youth-us-schools (accessed March 2018).
11. "American Varieties: The Midwest Accent," *Do You Speak American?*, PBS.org, http://www.pbs.org/speak/seatosea/americanvarieties/midwest/ (accessed March 2018).
12. Grace Kao, Elizabeth Vaquera, and Kimberly Goyette, *Education and Immigration* (Cambridge, UK: Polity Press, 2013).

Chapter 6
How to Combat Assimilation

1. Emily Greenman and Yu Xie, "Is Assimilation Theory Dead? The Effect of Assimilation on Adolescent Well-Being," *Social Science Research*, vol. 37, no. 1 (2008), https://doi.org/10.1016/j.ssresearch.2007.07.003.
2. Jay Patel, "To Assimilate or to Acculturate?" University of Maryland, 2012, http://www.english.umd.edu/interpolations/3460.
3. Ananya Mandal, "What Is Melanin," News-Medical.net, https://www.news-medical.net/health/What-is-Melanin.aspx (accessed March 2018).
4. Dennis O'Neil, "Skin Color Adaptation," *Human Biological Adaptability*, https://www2.palomar.edu/anthro/adapt/ adapt_4.htm (accessed March 2018).

Glossary

assimilation The process of becoming similar. In the context of cultural assimilation, it is the process of a minority group changing its customs and attitudes to become similar to the majority culture.

citizen A person living in a city or country with legal protection, privileges, and rights from their government.

code-switching Changing one's style of communication, language, appearance, or behavior based on the environment and social situation.

colonize To use power to take control of land and/or people in order to establish colonies or settlements, typically used in reference to European nations and migration across the world.

culture The behaviors, beliefs, and customs shared by a group of people. Culture can be further specified by ethnic, regional, age, or social groups, amongst others.

ethnicity An identity based on shared culture, ancestry, language, or customs such as Korean, Jewish, Hispanic or Latinx, Khmer, and Rohingya.

Eurocentric Mainly focused on Europe and Europeans, especially when considering history, culture, economics, and the arts.

immigrant A person who moves, or migrates, to another country for permanent residence.

majority/dominant culture A group of people that hold the most power, influence, and control in a society. Majority is not always based on numbers.

minority/subordinate culture A group of people that have less power, influence, and control in a society and are, as a result, disadvantaged. Minorities in the US include women, Muslims, people of color, and others.

race A categorization based on ancestry, culture, and physical characteristics that continues to change meaning over time, as determined by society. As of 2018, the US Census offers six races including white, Black or African American, American Indian or Alaska Native, Asian, and Native Hawaiian or Other Pacific Islander, and "Other Races." Hispanic and Latinx are considered ethnicities.

refugees People who have been forced to leave their home country typically to escape violence, war, and harassment.

xenophobia An intense fear, distrust, and hatred of people from different countries or cultures.

Further Reading

Books
Heads Up Sociology. New York, NY: DK Publishing, 2018.

Khan, Khizr. *This Is Our Constitution*. New York, NY: Alfred A. Knopf, 2017.

Levinson, Cynthia. *Fault Lines in the Constitution: The Framers, Their Fights, and the Flaws That Affect Us Today*. Atlanta, GA: Peachtree Publishers, 2017.

Osborne, Linda Barrett. *This Land Is Our Land: The History of American Immigration*. New York, NY: Abrams, 2016.

Websites

Fact Monster
www.factmonster.com
A search engine and online resource for students that offers homework help, games, quizzes, and more on a wide variety of topics.

History
www.history.com
A website from the History Channel that offers extensive historical facts and accounts.

Immigration Data & Statistics
www.dhs.gov/immigration-statistics
Detailed statistics and information regarding immigration, refugees, and more from the US Department of Homeland Security.

PBS Learning Media
www.pbslearningmedia.org
Multimedia platform that engages students and teachers on topics such as social studies, language arts, and the arts.

Index

A
accents, dialects, and speech patterns, 55–56, 60–61, 63, 66
acculturation, 62–64, 66
African Americans, 9, 44, 56
African American Vernacular English (AAVE), 56
American identity, 5, 18, 61
Angel Island, CA, 28
assimilation, 5–8, 10, 31, 41, 42–43, 44–46, 48, 50, 64, 67
Atlantic slave trade, 15–16

B
Blackish, 66
Brown v. Board of Education (1954), 40
bullying, 48, 53–54, 56

C
California Gold Rush (1848–1854), 26, 37
Calvo, Luz, 65
Carlisle Indian Industrial School, PA, 33–35
Cavanaugh, James Michael, 33
Cherokee people, 21–22
Chinese Exclusion Act of 1882, 26
Chou, Rosalind S., 43
Civil Rights Act (1964), 40
civil rights movement, 6, 40
Civil War (1861–1865), 24, 25, 39, 54
clothing, 45–46, 56
code-switching, 66
Columbus, Christopher, 10, 12, 14, 16, 21
The Cooking Gene (Twitty), 65
cultural assimilation, 5, 8, 9, 10, 18, 44, 45, 46, 48, 50–51, 53, 57, 59, 60, 62, 67, 69

D
Decolonize Your Diet (Calvo and Esuqibel), 65
deportation, 26, 37
discrimination, 6, 25, 36, 37, 40, 42, 45–46, 55, 56
Displaced Persons Act (1948), 32
dominant culture, 5, 9, 10, 18, 62, 64

E
Ellis Island, NY, 28
Emancipation Proclamation (1863), 24
English language, 21, 35–36, 56, 58–59, 61, 63
Erikson, Leif, 10
Esuqibel, Catriona Rueda, 65
Eurocentricity, 52, 54, 56, 61
Executive Order 9066 (Japanese internment), 37–38

F
Fair Housing Act of 1968, 40
Feagin, Joe R., 43
Fresh Off the Boat, 66

H
hair styles, 34, 56, 61, 69

I
immigration, 5, 26, 28–29, 58
Immigration Act of 1924, 31
Indian boarding schools, 31, 33–35
Indian Removal Act (1830), 21
indigenous people, 10, 12–13, 14, 34, 35
Indigenous Peoples' Day, 14
internalization, 59–61, 67
internment camps, 37–38, 42

J
Jackson, Andrew, 21–23
Jane the Virgin, 66

Examining Assimilation

Japanese internment, 37–38, 42, 43
The Jemima Code: Two Centuries of African American Cookbooks (Tipton-Martin), 65
Jennings, Jazz, 47
Jewish, anti-sentiment, 46
Jim Crow laws, 38–40, 44
Johnson, Lyndon B., 40

K
Kennedy, John F., 10

L
Latinx, anti-sentiment, 36–37
LGBTQ, anti-sentiment, 54–55
LGBTQ culture, 47–49
Lincoln, Abraham, 24–25, 54
Louisiana Purchase, 19, 20

M
media, 50–53, 66
melanin, 67
The Melting Pot (Zangwill), 5
Mendez, Sylvia, 37
Mexican-American War (1846–1848), 23–24
Mexicans, anti-sentiment, 23, 25, 36–37
The Mindy Project, 66
model minorities, 42, 44
music, 63
Muslim, anti-sentiment, 45–46
The Myth of the Model Minority: Asian Americans Facing Racism (Chou and Feagin), 43–44

N
Nakao, Annie, 43
names, 42, 50, 55, 56–58, 61
A Nation of Immigrants (Kennedy), 10
Native Americans, anti-sentiment, 12, 20–22, 31, 33, 34

Nativism, 30, 31

P
passing as white, 44
Phạm, Vy H`ông, 57, 58
Pratt, Richard H., 33
prejudice, 30, 45, 46, 48, 53, 61

R
racism, 40, 53, 61
Refugee Act of 1980, 32
refugees, 7, 9, 32, 41, 58, 62
religious assimilation, 44–45
repatriation, 37
Roosevelt, Theodore, 26, 30, 31

S
school, 53–57
segregation, 36, 39–40, 44, 54
Sherman, Sean, 65
The Sioux Chef's Indigenous Kitchen (Sherman), 65
slavery, 15–16, 19, 24–25, 38, 39
stereotypes, 42, 45, 52–53, 54, 66

T
13th Amendment (1865), 25, 38–39
Tipton-Martin, Toni, 65
Trail of Tears, 23
Treaty of Guadalupe Hidalgo, 19, 23
Twitty, Michael W., 65

U
US Constitution, 17–18, 19, 23, 28, 45

V
Voting Rights Act (1965), 40

X
xenophobia, 30

Z
Zangwill, Israel, 5